CHARLES PERRAULT

THE VINDICATION OF WIVES

TRANSLATED FROM THE FRENCH BY
ROLAND GANT

WITH ILLUSTRATIONS BY
CLAUSS

Miniature Books

RODALE BOOKS INC.

FIRST PUBLISHED 1954
BY RODALE BOOKS INC.
EMMAUS, PENNSYLVANIA, AND
LONDON, ENGLAND

COPYRIGHT IN ENGLAND 1954
BY J. I. RODALE

MANUFACTURED IN ENGLAND

THE VINDICATION OF WIVES

A NOTE ON CHARLES PERRAULT

THE Perraults were a *bourgeois* family, typical of many who contributed to France's glory in the Golden Age of Louis XIV. Rendering valuable service to both court and government they were, on the other hand, both respected and admired by the common people.

Charles Perrault was born in Paris on 12 January 1628, the son of Pierre Perrault, a barrister. There were four other sons who distinguished themselves in the careers they chose. Pierre became Receiver General of Paris, Jean became a lawyer, Nicolas was an eminent theologian and Claude a brilliant doctor and architect. Claude Perrault used his influence on behalf of the poet Boileau at the Sorbonne (which did not prevent Boileau from attacking Charles Perrault in one of the most famous literary quarrels of all time), and it was Claude who designed the Colonnade du Louvre, the church of St. Germain l'Auxerrois and the Observatoire in Paris. He possessed an ordered genius, great vision coupled to a strong creative urge, and boundless curiosity about mankind and the world in which he lived. Curiosity was, in fact, the death of this extraordinary man who was responsible for some of the most remarkable buildings in Paris. He died in 1688 from a disease which it was believed he had contracted whilst dissecting the body of a camel in the Jardin du Roi.

Charles Perrault began his education at the college of Beauvais and intended to become a philosopher. One day, after an argument with his tutor, he walked out, followed by his friend Beaurain, and together they went up to the Luxembourg Gardens where, in the shade of the trees, they swore never to return to college but to continue their studies independent of tutors and rigid curriculum. 'We carried out our resolution,' Perrault recorded, 'and for three or four years M. Beaurain came to my home twice nearly every day—from eight to eleven in the morning and from three to five in the afternoon. If I possess any knowledge I owe it chiefly to those three or four years of study. We read almost all of the Bible, nearly all Tertullian, *De l'habillement des femmes*; we read Virgil, Horace, Tacitus and most of the classical authors, making extracts which I still have.'

With Beaurain, and his brothers Claude and Nicolas, Charles collaborated to produce an *Enéide travestie* but, although he had begun to write whilst a very young man, it was as a lawyer that he graduated at Orléans in 1651. He became clerk to his brother Pierre, the Receiver General, and held this government appointment for ten years, from 1654 to 1664, before being appointed adviser on artistic matters by Louis XIV's great Controller General of Finance, Jean Baptiste Colbert. He was made a member of the Académie française in 1671 and was popular, not only because of his wit and amiability but also for his efficient handling of the business side of the Académie.

It was inevitable that some people should be jealous of a man who had such close relations with court and government and when Charles Perrault read before the members of the Académie a poem entitled *Le Siècle de Louis le Grand* on 27 January 1687, he aroused the fury of some of his literary contemporaries and touched off an intellectual wrangle that went on for years and spread to every country in Europe. The poem was an attempt to prove the superiority of modern writers over the ancients and it was attacked and ridiculed by Racine and Boileau. Perrault replied to the attacks with *Parallèle des anciens et des modernes*—a work in four volumes, and a question which had long been discussed by philosophers and scholars, including Bacon and Descartes, now developed into the renowned 'quarrel between the ancients and the moderns' with Perrault as champion of the moderns and Boileau as champion of the ancients.

The Vindication of Wives (*l'Apologie des Femmes*) was published in 1694 in reply to Boileau's *Réflexions sur Longin*, and so the quarrel went on, gathering force and spreading to England where Jonathan Swift wrote his prose satire on the subject and called it *The Battle of the Books*. This was published in 1704 by which time Perrault and Boileau had already been reconciled for four years.

After the death of Colbert in 1687, Charles Perrault devoted himself to writing and, perhaps as an echo of *Le Siècle de Louis le Grand* and the arguments it had provoked, he produced a series of short biographies entitled *Les Hommes illustres qui ont paru en France pendant ce siècle, avec leurs portraits en nature*, now mostly remembered by the illustrations. He was already quite old when he wrote his *Mother Goose's Tales* but, although they were originally intended as passing amusements for children, the delicacy, wit, and originality of style made an imperishable gallery of Red Riding Hood, Puss in Boots, Cinderella, Blue Beard, and the Sleeping Beauty ensuring that Perrault's name will never be forgotten. He himself might be surprised to find he is remembered for these stories two and a half centuries later when his other work is no longer read and his quarrel with Boileau has cooled to an episode in the pages of histories of literature.

Almost everyone knows the fairy tales but few can have read Perrault's other work and almost nothing of it has been translated into English. This first English edition of *l'Apologie des Femmes* therefore introduces a new aspect of Charles Perrault and is an echo of the battle-cry of the champion of the moderns. ROLAND GANT

THE VINDICATION OF WIVES

TIMANDER had a son. Who so morose
And misanthropically bellicose?
He raged against mankind with all his might,
Loosed on his neighbours his sarcastic spite,
And on the Fair Sex, caustically keen,
Would exercise the sourness of his spleen.

His father, wishing that the family name
Should be borne on through centuries of fame,

[11]

A hundred times entreated him to take
A wife, if only for the family's sake.
A hundred times he stood aghast to see
His son in anger brush aside the plea.

Finding the boy less choleric one day,
The father drew him on one side to say:
'Woman charms man; how then can one man's son
Deny her virtues or her graces shun?
May I not hope to see you spurn Disdain
And turn a convert to the Sex again?
If, through some holy grace, you should ignore
Earth's charms, to fix your eyes on Heaven's the more,
'Twould be unjust to blame so just a cause,
Such sacrifice would merit my applause,
But here it is the madness of a fool,
Not virtue, turns you from tradition's rule.'

'Tis an eternal rule on Nature's part,—
And one engraved on every human heart—
To hand down to our sons the blessed light,
That gift in which our forebears all unite,
Which right and custom both combine to bless
And to withhold is purely selfishness.
Men may to immortality aspire,
And win it, too, my son, through sweet desire.
Can you, then, contemplate with unconcern
A child who would love God, be loved in turn,
And might, when death has closed your eyes at last,
Add future honours to your noble past?

From him would spring a second race, by whom
You would be honoured till the day of doom.

Unfaithful wives there are and not exempt
From proper censure—they deserve contempt;
But just because of one or two who err,
Must the whole sex accept the general slur?

In a great City where all kinds abound,
Each man's acquaintances are made and found

According to the tastes that are his own.
(For by his inclinations Man is known)
Everyone finds, no matter where he is,
Others who own to similarities.
He who by learning has acquired renown
Finds men as wise as he somewhere in town,

And he who tries to be an Alchemist,
And, trying, only turns his gold to mist,
Falls among those who help melt gold away,
And hastens to the poor-house the same way.
The music lover goes about to find
The nice ear and the music-loving mind,

[15]

And he who gives his nose a ruby glow
Has friends with even rosier ones to show.
The pious who respond to God's appeal,
Love only those who boast an equal zeal,
And on whose friendship Heaven sets the seal,
Yet men pronounce, by the few women they meet,
Damnation universal and complete!

For six without brains and devoid of charm,
Who at all costs provoke much chatter and harm,
By their dancing, their games and masquerades,
Their indiscreet gifts and their wretched parades,
A thousand others exist, good and sincere,
And of their tranquil lives we nothing hear.

At all times and places you'll find the Coquette,
At every Amusement she's bound to be met,
Go to the Opera, to the Court or a Ball,
To the Fair, on her your eye's bound to fall.
It would seem, to watch her mad, flighty chase,
That she is legion to be at each place.
Of women a hundred not two we know
Would agree to be seen in places so low.

Reject then, my son, this maxim unfair
That a worthy woman is all too rare,
This is the talk of a man who seduces,
And of brazen women a long list produces
As examples to his Iris display
An inducement to her to fall the same way.

Instead of visiting these haunts of pleasure
To feast your eyes and while away your leisure
At the Tuileries and at Court parades,
On painted cheeks and bejewelled brocades,

[17]

Go into hospitals where there are lying
Suffering patients, the dead and the dying;
At all times of the day you can meet there,
Despite the infection polluting the air,
A thousand lovely women who are seen,
Their beauty hid 'neath humility's screen,
Who in their piety have wondrous charms
That are unknown in coquettes' shameless arms.

[18]

Look in this attic, through this cellar door,
In all the nooks where swarm a thousand Poor;
A score of virtuous women you will meet
Who in pity go into each dark retreat.
With love and zeal their duties they fulfil,
With boundless charity they tend each ill.
Among the humble folk in every house
Maiden and mother work until the spouse

[19]

Comes tired at night (their labour all for him),
Knowing they live to gratify each whim.
Won over by their conduct quiet and wise,
Your harsh opinions you will soon revise.

Do you not know that all Civility
Is born in Women with propriety?
That in them all politeness is innate,
Gentleness, taste and manners delicate?
Look, if you will, at each uncivil wight
Who lives alone, from women shut up tight,
You'll find him filthy, mannerless and wild,
A boor in manner and in speech defiled.
To him a finer thought quite strange has grown,
He only speaks harsh words and saws well known.
All good for him is buried and long dead,
And at our modern ways he jeers instead.
In testing, all of value must be old,
Such varied talents form the Pedant's mould,
Most irksome, loathsome and withal purblind
Of any creature known to all mankind.

When foolish women in so light a way
Devote themselves to singing and trifling play,
Are you not sometimes tempted to exclaim
That it is husbands who are oft to blame,
By the excess of their rule severe?
Through indolence or the too mild course they steer?

Should you one day, according to my wish,
The thought of married state begin to relish,

[20]

You must not try to dictate to your bride
And like a Pedagogue then live in pride,
Love and respect are witness to a true esteem
In husbands a conduct which should be supreme:
Of women it has everywhere been said
That haughtiness is in them all inbred;
Each woman in her man a master seeks
When by his virtue his command he speaks;
And when she acts with high imperious hand,
'Tis the weakling husband who can't command.

In certain marriages are sometimes seen
Such unwise spouses who themselves demean;
But who would dare to murmur of deceit
When they in courtship never tried to meet?
But, like their parents, who through glasses read
For months on end each article and deed,
Each petty point they by law contract,
Gold and silver shared out before they act,
Without ensuring that they do commit
A pair to unite both different age and wit.
For felicitous living they do not see
That the choice of each one must be left free;
This truth is one for all about to wed,
But it does not enter a Miser's head.

When the first man came into the universe,
With power to command all living things diverse,
With complacency he no doubt observed
The power and riches for himself reserved;

But awakening from sleep at last to life
His eyes by God were opened on his wife,
His other half, companion of his days;
So, turning from all else on her to gaze,
He then decided in her heart to reign
Were better than earth's master to remain.

We ready victims fall to Fame's allure,
The power and charm of Gold is all too sure,

[23]

Despite the dazzling sparkle they present,
There is one thing that brooks no precedent,
Which is to find one's future closely tied
To the future of a mannered, gentle bride,
Whose Dowry is enhanced by a nature chaste,
In her, virtue and warmth are interlaced.
And if to this Heaven was pleased to add
The gift of beauty so that she is clad
In comeliness, and to this perfection
Are joined fine features and pink complexion;
If her eyes, set below an ivory brow,
With a radiant sweetness burn and glow;
And if a coral mouth beyond compare
With lips whose form begs a smile to wear;
And her rosy hand rivals that of Dawn,
With fingertips that are still pinker drawn:
Should we then deplore such a Husband's fate,
And would you not envy him such a mate?

There's nothing merits more envy on earth,
No part of life which holds more golden worth;
Most dire misfortunes are easy to bear,
When two hearts are joined together to share;
The very smallest joy that Heaven sends
Like a sea of pleasure before them extends.

If a husband recklessly squanders wealth
In wild dissipation and damages his health.
By careful housekeeping and the frugal meal,
A Wife turns him adroitly from woe to weal,

[24]

And from his wildness weans him with success
Until the day when he eschews all excess.

　　Should she discover there's some gallant affair,
She makes herself still more gentle and fair,
Bearing in silence 'til he does forswear
All dalliance, and touched, goes back to her care.
Through such women as these fickle youth renounces
All previous looseness and all vice denounces:
Her example the family peace regains,
Servants she directs and children restrains,

A decadent House she thus does nourish,
Through her 'tis revived once more to flourish.

It is not only in the first fine days,
Nor in the ardours of youthful embrace,
But in marriage where lie delight and joy
Which last from the outset and do not cloy,
A way of which happiness is the prize.

Ah! What contentment is seen in the eyes
Of a husband, who in sick-bed confined,
Is nursed by a wife with no thought in mind
But to tend to his needs and his pain to ease
And weeps in secret if she danger sees;
Physic tastes sweeter with comfort and cheer
When 'tis proffered to him by hands so dear;
And if at last Heaven his death requires
In her arms without murmur he expires.

Such is the peaceful and fortunate lot
Of he who in marriage has tied the knot,
Whereas the free bachelor ends his life
Locked on his bed with death in mortal strife,
Through panic and confusion as he dies,
His servant steals—through half-closed eyes
He sees, and senses through stupor and pain
The theft of the sheet upon which he is lain.

If a faithful servant granted him by fate
Had been there to ease his desolate state,

Then with faithless friends he would have been cursed,
And worse, relations crowding all athirst
For his property and trembling there in fear
Of his will, seek the Confessor and the Lawyer's ear;
In mortal fear that quinine will no more revive
And not for long enough will he survive.

 Is it not true, my son, that such a portrait
Of the tender joys of the married state,
And that all the horrors of bachelorhood
Obsess you, upset you, and vanquish your mood?
By what I have told you your mind is moved,
And to you at last the right road has proved.
I think I know the decision that you'll make
But to muse on it more time you may take.

CPSIA information can be obtained at www.ICGtesting.com
Printed in the USA
BVOW09s2044080916

461556BV00004B/62/P